Wake Yourself Up!

How to Push Through Your Problems and Go for Your Dreams

by Alana Leone

Cover Design by Cathi Stevenson

Editing by Maura Leon

Proofreading by Heather Taylor

Interior Design by Rudy Milanovich

ISBN: 978-0-9968547-8-8

Published by
Pushy Coaching LTD

Dedication

This book is dedicated to my amazing children. Everything I do, I do for them. A person could not love someone more than I love my children. They are my biggest inspiration — my *why*.

Acknowledgements

I acknowledge God as my rock, my family, my friends, every book, every sunset, and every experience. I would not be who I am without everyone and everything.

Contents

Introduction

A STATE OF CONFUSION

Once upon a time, a little girl was born. Like most little girls, she came into the world filled with love and happiness.

During her childhood, however, a spell was cast, and the little girl fell into a deep sleep. As she slept, her feelings of love and happiness turned into guilt and shame.

This was a spell of confusion; the little girl had no idea that she was asleep. She walked and talked, went to school, grew up, and had a child of her own, never knowing what was really going on.

***

As you may have guessed, that little girl was me. From a very young age, I was in a sleep state.

I could have spent my entire life in that state of confusion, never knowing who I really was or doing what I really wanted to do. Fortunately, however, I managed to wake myself up and push through to the amazing life that I'm living today.

AN INVITATION

Once I got myself out of the sleep state, I discovered that I wasn't the only one who'd been walking around under a spell. There were many other sleepwalkers, some who still had no idea what was going on and others who were just starting to awaken.

And that's why I wrote this book.

While the details may be different, our stories are very much the same: the ups and downs, the hopes and fears, the complexity and the confusion.

You're reading this now because you are ready to wake yourself up. You may not have known that you were sleeping, but you do now.

You also may not have known that you helped me to complete this book. Every time I didn't feel like writing or life appeared to be getting in the way, I thought of you, and that thought kept me going. I knew that if I could help you to have a better day, a better hour, or even a better minute, then I had to share my truth.

You can take what you like and leave the rest; all I ask is that you consider each piece with an open mind. I'll be asking you questions that others may not have asked, and I invite you to answer with complete self-honesty.

Will you allow me to push you a little?

I'm willing to push you because I know that you're worth it. And I want you to know it too.

Deep down, you already do.

Beneath all the pain, anger, guilt, shame, resentment, fear, and self-loathing, you know who you really are and what you're here to do.

Writing this book brought me right back to all of those feelings in me. I remembered not only *how* I took the steps to change my life, but also *why* I did it.

As you read this book, I want you to discover your why; it will give you the strength to overcome any obstacle.

AN OPPORTUNITY

While on the surface this may look like a quick and easy read, there's a much deeper experience available to you. Take your time, ponder each question, consider everything presented (*especially* if it's something that you've never considered before), and your results will be life-changing.

At the end of each chapter, you'll find an opportunity for group or family discussion on the subject that you've just completed. If you have one or more people in your life with whom you can share this process, congratulations! You are very fortunate.

If, on the other hand, you're doing it on your own, then you'll simply be writing your answers in a journal rather than sharing them out loud.

Don't skip this step. By the time you finish the book, you'll understand why it was an important part of the process.

Finding others to go through this with you is not necessary. You can get just as much value on your own. And if you are the only person who creates a life worth living by actually *doing* this book instead of just reading it, then every minute that I put into it will have been worth it.

As you hold this book in your hands right now, ask yourself:

Will I allow myself to receive this gift?

Will I allow myself to participate fully?

Let's find out…

Chapter One
The Wounding

ENERGY AND VIBRATION

Have you ever thought about the full cycle of life?

Have you ever really sat and wondered:

What is the purpose of being born, becoming a teenager, entering adulthood, aging, and then dying?

Is it for a higher purpose or just for us to survive and die?

As a child, I thought nothing of these things. I thought only of myself.

In the beginning, the input that I received wasn't through words as much as it was from the energy and vibration of the people around me.

As I grew, I learned to respond to:

- What I was told
- What I heard around me
- Body language
- Energy (for example, the feeling of "walking on eggshells")

This information came from:

- Parents
- Family
- Teachers
- Other people in the community
- Television
- Music

Think about it:

Where did your input come from?

FROM GENERATION TO GENERATION

Even with our parents meaning the best for us, loving us, and being all that they can be, they can only be all that they *know how* to be. Their energy is part of their parents' energy, which has been passed down from generation to generation by their ancestors before them.

This energy can include positive things, such as:

- Love
- Drive
- Perseverance

And at the same time, it can include negatives, like:

- Shame
- Guilt
- Self-loathing

Our parents' experiences have also been influenced by their teachers, other family members, and friends. It's all part of a pattern.

In the beginning, what got passed on to me was:

- Love and happiness
- Guilt and shame

Think about it:

What got passed on to you?

YOUR LIFE STORY

While your story may be different from mine, I want you to understand that the experiences you have throughout your lifetime happen for a reason—a bigger reason than you might be able to understand while you're going through those experiences. It may not be until you have an eye-opening or heart-opening experience that you begin to question the meaning of your life.

Once you start questioning, you will discover that you have all of your experiences so that you can find the purpose that is meant for you and become exactly who you were born to be.

Let me explain.

I was born for a purpose. As an infant, I was born into love. Up to about the age of two, I remember feeling the love.

Then, something changed. I didn't know exactly what it was, but it stayed with me.

Today, looking back, I know the truth of who I was as a young child.

I was full of:

- Innocence
- Wonder
- Unconditional love

Just look at the face of a child under the age of three. Or if you can, find a picture of yourself at the age of two or three.

What do you see?

I was:

- Powerful
- Knowing
- Sweet
- Funny
- Loving

And then, the wounding set in.

It sets in at different ages for different people. For some, it's right from birth, and for others, it's later.

Regardless of when it happens, though, the wounding becomes your life story.

Think about it:

What qualities did you have as a child?

How has the wounding become your life story?

SURVIVAL MODE

At a very young age, I went from feeling love to feeling chaos and confusion. I was so confused that I instantly went inward.

I didn't like pain.

I didn't like shame.

I felt like I didn't know anything, but the one thing I did know was that I had to get away from the pain.

(Of course, it has taken years of personal development for me to understand all of this.)

Having shifted fully into survival mode, from the age of three on, I chose the role of the victim.

Everything happened *to* me.

All I could think about was that I was hurt and broken.

I searched for fulfillment from outside sources and got nothing but more confusion.

And once the cycle of searching and confusion began, it seemed to get deeper and faster as time went on.

I started…

…acting out.

…bullying children.

…experimenting with booze and drugs.

All of this was happening at the age of ten.

I was hurt and confused, with no tools to stop the pain. So to help myself feel better, I became the pain to others.

When that didn't work to stop the pain, I spiraled down into more and more trouble.

Think about it:

How have you responded to confusion or pain?

How has that worked out for you?

THE FIRST DECISION

There are points in every person's life at which they make a decision, and that decision impacts the rest of their life. Whether you remember your decisions or not, they were made.

My first decision, I remember, was about money. Because most of the yelling and fighting was about money, I decided that I must make a lot of money. Then, there would be no pain.

It seemed simple, so that was the choice that I made.

Then came my second decision.

It seemed like no matter how hard I tried to be good and nice, everyone kept telling me that I was bad.

At that point, I could have chosen to be really bad or really good.

I chose bad.

I thought to myself:

Screw it. I am checking out.

Think about it:

What was your first decision?

What decisions did you make after that?

MAKING EXCUSES

I remember a story that was told to me by a friend:

A pair of twins shared:

- *The same parents*
- *The same school*
- *The same extracurricular activities*

One twin became a doctor.

The other was a bum on the street.

When the twins were interviewed in separate rooms where neither could hear the other, they both said the same thing:

"With parents like mine, what would you expect me to become?"

I found this story interesting.

When we don't realize that we are making choices and living our lives based on decisions that we made as early as the first few years of our lives, we end up making excuses about why we are the way that we are.

Instead, we could be…

…searching to find out how to become successful with the experiences that we've had.

…clearing the reaction thought that resulted in that choice at such a young age.

…coming up with a different choice as an adult.

Think about it:

What excuses have you made about yourself?

How can you become successful with the experiences that you've had?

How can you clear your earliest reaction thoughts?

How would you now, as a functional adult, make a healthy choice?

THE SLEEP STATE

Having decided that since everyone was telling me I was bad, I would be the greatest bad person they had ever seen, off I went to follow that path.

This led me to:

- Alcohol and hard drugs
- Youth detention centers
- Hardcore friends
- A life of crime and self-loathing

A child's concept of reality can be quite amazing when you start looking at it from a new perspective. Your early choices, made with little or no conscious awareness on your part, secure the outward fulfillment of the negative energy (such as shame and guilt) that has been passed down to you over generations.

In the process, you get more pain piled on top of what was already there, and you go deeper and deeper into the sleep state of your lack of conscious awareness.

This sleep state can last…

…one year.

…two years.

…five years.

…twenty years.

If you did nothing to wake yourself up, it could last for your entire life.

Think about it:

How did your early choices secure the fulfillment of negative energy that was passed down to you?

How long has your sleep state lasted?

Have you done anything to wake yourself up?

A MOMENT OF CLARITY

I always wondered why the world was filled with:

- Crime
- Addiction
- Diseases

I can now see it as clear as day.

Everyone wants to do better and be better.

But how?

While most people say that they're willing to do something about their situation, sadly, few ever do.

In choosing to be bad, I chose:

- Drugs and alcohol
- Bad boys
- Anything else that could make me forget my pain

From the ages of thirteen to twenty-one, I spiraled out of control.

Then, a glimpse of awakening happened.

I realized that the lifestyle I'd been living was beginning to feel like too much pain.

And I recognized that I was running from pain because I didn't know how to process it into something understandable.

In a moment of clarity, I asked myself:

What can I do to get out of this pain?

I had tried a lot of different strategies.

Things like:

- Drinking only vodka instead of rye
- Partying only on weekends

These were my methods of coping. I was using the only skills that I could muster.

Then, I came up with a whole new solution.

It was perfect!

So that I could have someone to love, I was going to have a baby. This was going to stop the pain; I just knew it.

(As I mentioned, I kept running into pain because I did not have a great decision-making model to follow. My solutions were impulsive, and while this did end up being the best decision I could have made, I do not recommend having a baby as a way to get out of pain.)

Think about it:

What have you wondered about the world?

When have you had a moment of clarity?

What have you recognized about your life?

What coping methods have you used?

SEVEN MORE YEARS

So…

I had my beautiful daughter.

I went to AA.

I was doing well.

Even though it ended up taking me another try, I came back again and got my life straight. I started thinking about helping others. Having spent my entire life only thinking of myself, this was a whole new concept for me.

I was awakening.

I started taking parenting classes.

I started reading books about people's experiences and the tools they were using to be better for the world.

I really got into life.

I discovered counseling.

I went back to school.

I had another gorgeous daughter.

Because I kept getting healthier, I thought that as a family, everything was perfect.

In reality, home life was still hectic, and I was still angry.

As I learned tools (however small) to cope, things got progressively better. At one point, they got so good that it felt like my girls and I had the world by the tail.

And then, it happened again.

In spite of doing all of this work to make my life better, I went back to sleep — for seven more years.

When I look back on this time, I still feel a little shocked at how fast life can change.

How did this happen?

While I certainly don't have all the answers, one thing I do know is that life is a process. It's a process of doing a little better every day.

Life will happen no matter what.

There will be:

- Ups and downs
- Twists and turns

I believe that the purpose of these things is to make us exactly who we are at this moment in time, and and I believe that it is all perfect.

I feel so blessed to have had all of the experiences that I've had.

And I really love the person I am.

Think about it:

How have you gotten healthier?

Do you think about others?

What tools have you learned to help you cope?

Have you ever felt like you had the world by the tail, only to fall asleep again?

Do you feel blessed to have had the experiences that you've had?

Do you love the person you are?

Family or Group Discussion:

Take turns discussing your experiences, thoughts, and feelings about the wounding, then answer the following questions for yourself:

What is your first step toward creating the life you want to live?

When will you take that step?

Chapter Two
Forgiveness

THE EASY WAY?

Everything that happens to you and all of the lessons you learn are for the purpose of adding value to your life, so that you can become the truly enlightened being you are meant to be.

Until you consciously realize this, you will continue to be asleep in confusion.

While it may seem like staying asleep would be easier, it is actually the harder road to follow. When your consciousness is asleep, you are like a robot.

You survive, each day, to the best of your ability.

You don't strive to make a difference.

Even though every once-in-a-while you have a brief awakening to your purpose, after trying it out for a short time...

...you realize that doing things differently takes work.

...you think that it's too hard.

...you end up quitting on yourself.

In the short term, this looks easier.

Then, along come experiences like:

- Heartbreak
- Sickness
- Poverty
- Divorce

Think about it:

Have you ever felt like it might just be easier to stay asleep?

In what ways have you been like a robot?

How many times have you quit on yourself?

What kinds of experiences have you gone through as a result?

A HIGHER STATE

When you wake yourself up by pushing through your comfort zone until the discomfort becomes comfortable, you are raising yourself to a new, higher state.

The energetic vibration is actually higher.

While it does take work, your choice to move forward brings you:

- More opportunities
- Overflowing love for yourself and others
- Health
- Wealth

The higher up the mountain you climb, the more of the good stuff you will get.

Sadly, however, many of us don't realize that if we just push through our beliefs and fears, we'll find people to help us along. We don't know that those people are out there for us.

What if no one has ever taught you…

…that failing is actually an important part of success?

…that if you practice the wrong thing, then "practice, practice, practice" doesn't work?

What if your little light inside wants to shine, but the tools to make that happen have never been provided to you?

Sometimes, we just don't know what we don't know.

Think about it:

What opportunities could you create by choosing to become comfortable with your discomfort?

How much more could you accomplish if you were willing to fail?

What could you achieve if you knew the right thing to practice?

How bright would your light be if you had the tools to really let it shine?

HURTS AND MISPERCEPTIONS

We've all had things that were hard to forgive.

We all have stories about how people…

…hurt us.

…were mean and angry.

…ruined our lives.

Have you ever considered that those people…

…were doing the absolute best that they could with their hurts, experiences, and perceptions?

…were in pain and didn't know what to do with the pain, so they lashed out?

Have you ever lashed out at your spouse or children when you had a bad day?

While the severity of these situations may seem different, the process is the same. Depending on our level of pain and our ability to cope, we've all experienced some degree of hurting other people with our words and actions.

Think about it:

What stories do you have about people who have
done you wrong?

What types of pain might they have been
experiencing?

When have your words or actions hurt people?

What hurts or misperceptions were you experiencing at the time?

CHOOSING YOUR TRUTH

Here's a challenging question:

Do you feel in your heart that you could experience compassion toward a rapist or a murderer?

Think about this:

What's the difference between you and that person?

Could the difference be as slight as a single moment — the moment in which they made that split-second decision to commit the act?

Let's look at something more personal.

Maybe you have a story about your childhood involving parents, guardians, or other family members.

"They ruined my life," you might say.

By saying such a thing...

...you give all of your power to those people.

...you take no responsibility for your part in the situation.

The part that I'm talking about is forgiveness.

What if you were to change the negative thought to a positive thought?

Which thought feels better?

Which thought are you willing to accept?

If every situation is neutral until your thought gives it fuel, then couldn't the positive thought be just as true as the negative thought?

Who decides what's true and what's not true in your life?

Are you a hundred percent sure that they ruined your life?

I'm not saying that our parents don't have responsibility for their actions. They choose their lives for themselves, and they can choose to get healthy or not.

But their decisions have nothing to do with us.

Think about it:

Have you ever acted on a split-second bad decision?

Have you ever given up your power by not being willing to forgive?

What negative thoughts could you benefit from changing to positive ones?

NO REGRETS

You get one chance at life. Whether you make it successful or not, you will have to live with it.

When you are at death's door, will you have regrets?

I believe that people who don't strive to be better have more regrets.

That's one of the reasons why I push myself in my own life. I don't want to have regrets when it's too late to do anything about them.

When I'm in my rocking chair at the age of 110, I want to be able to say that I did my best at the game of life — that I really put in an honest effort.

Who could regret that?

Think about it:

What regrets do you have at this point in your life?

What can you do about them?

THE GIFT OF PEACE

Forgiveness is an integral part of your life's success. When you don't forgive others, it's like you're keeping a poison inside your body.

Forgiveness can come more easily when you practice:

- Understanding
- Empathy
- Compassion

That's what it means to live from your heart.

Because the poison of resentment and anger will, over time, promote disease in your body, forgiving others is actually a gift to yourself.

Take a moment, right now, and think about someone you've had a hard time forgiving.

Now, I want you to believe with all your heart — even if it's just for a quick minute — that to forgive that person, after all this time, is actually a gift to you, not to them.

They may not even know that you harbor unforgiveness toward them.

They may not even care.

The peace in your life is the beautifully wrapped gift for you.

My goal with this statement is for you to experience (even if it's just for one second):

- A glimmer of peace
- A soft spot
- Maybe even a smirk on your face

If you cannot muster a softness at all, then be easy on yourself, and realize that this process takes time.

Think about it:

How committed are you to living from your heart by practicing understanding, empathy, and compassion?

Could your body be healthier if you were more forgiving?

How much more peaceful would your life be if you were willing to give yourself the gift of forgiveness?

A LEGACY OF FREEDOM

Ask yourself:

Could unforgiveness be holding me back from everything that I want in my life?

Could forgiveness be the single most important thing I could do for myself and my posterity?

I believe that it could be.

Forgiveness opens the gate.

Remember that you have choices. You decide what you're willing to do.

The more that you search for freedom…

…the more freedom you'll have in your life.

…the more freedom your children will have in their lives.

…the more freedom there will be in the lives of your generations to come.

It really is worth it!

Think about it:

How has unforgiveness held you back from getting what you want in your life?

What are you willing to do to experience more freedom in your life?

How would it feel to leave a legacy of freedom to your generations to come?

Family or Group Discussion:

Take turns discussing your experiences, thoughts, and feelings about forgiveness, then answer the following questions for yourself:

What is your next step toward creating the life you want to live?

When will you take that step?

Chapter Three
Healing

SETTING FIRE TO YOUR PAST

Living your story all these years has involved pain and sacrifice.

Isn't it time for you to acknowledge yourself as a survivor?

You are strong and competent.

Celebrate who you are!

At this time in your life, you can make the choice to set fire to the past with forgiveness and love.

Then, you can:

- Look back
- Pick through the rubble
- Find the gifts
- See what you've learned

Imagine…

Through the charred remains and the smell of smoky debris, you pick up a dismantled picture.

Under the picture, you find an elegant and perfect gift.

The gift is wrapped in gold and red, with a bow so spectacular, there are no words to describe its beauty.

You open the gift.

With tears in your eyes, you remember the pain.

Then, you smile as you realize:

That story is your past.

Think about it:

What kinds of pain and sacrifice has your story involved?

How does it feel to acknowledge yourself as a survivor?

Are you ready to set fire to your past?

What gifts will you find in the rubble?

A BLANK CANVAS

Now that you've left the pain behind you, you can...

...say "thank you" to the past.

...make a decision to live in the present.

...fulfill your God-given purpose.

This is your reason for being here on Earth.

Now...the excitement starts!

You are standing in front of a blank canvas, and right beside you is a rich palette of experience and wisdom. Your brush will do whatever you instruct it to do.

What do you want to create?

The world is yours.

While the process of gaining clarity on what you want may take time and resources, whatever you want really is possible.

Instead of just surviving, you can now choose to truly live.

Think about it:

What will you gain by saying "thank you" to your past?

What does it mean to live fully in the present?

What if whatever you want really is possible?

How will you choose to fulfill your God-given purpose?

BREAKING THE CHAINS

My story was shame.

I was ashamed even to be heard…

…or seen.

…or loved.

I turned to drugs to escape the pain—or so I thought.

Being so young and naïve, little did I know that I was only piling on more hurt and more shame.

Your mind can be so deceitful and tricky to your heart and to your soul. It will set out to destroy you, one moment at a time, when the subconscious emotions of the past are stuffed down so far that you have no idea what is actually running you.

I was not taught tools to recover from rejection or betrayal; I was only taught about the hurt and the pain of the generations before me. It got handed down to each generation.

If I had not noticed what was really going on, then the chains would never have been broken.

To be truly free, I had to take a stand to break the chains of bondage.

Think about it:

What was your story?

What tools were you never taught?

Are you taking a stand to break the chains?

IT'S OKAY TO FEEL

Addictions of all kinds are epidemic in our world today.

There are…

…housewives at home with their children, taking prescription drugs to cope with the pain in their lives.

…lawyers and doctors at safe injection sites, shooting up drugs to cope with the pain of this world.

…people overeating to escape from their pain.

Just in writing this right now, I have a voice in my soul, yelling:

People…STOP!

It's okay to feel.

What are we doing?

There appears to be a feel-pain-and-push-it-away epidemic.

We must push *through* this generational load.

We must heal for our children.

Will you take a step?

Think about it:

Have you been a part of the feel-pain-and-push-it-away epidemic?

What have you used to escape the pain?

What if it really is okay to feel?

What would it be like to push *through*?

REMEMBERING YOUR INNOCENCE

You can begin with small baby steps. And it helps to have someone beside you who understands that all experiences are a chance to heal and to serve.

People can be so self-absorbed.

Notice how often you use these words:

- *My* pain
- *My* hurt
- Why *me*? It's not fair.

I understand that it's your pain; now, let's see the bigger picture of it all. Let's see the reason.

I realize that you may not have been taught this way.

I'm sharing with you now to open:

- Your eyes
- Your ears
- Your heart

Can you feel that?

It's the feeling of awakening.

It's the awareness that there are answers available to help you heal.

The essence of who you are is complete love.

Can you sit with that for one moment?

Remember the truth.

You were born:

- Innocent
- Beautiful
- A miracle

Remember that truth for one second in your heart.

Turn off your mind for one second, and sit in the warmth of your heart, remembering your innocence.

Close your eyes, and feel that hope and love.

Think about it:

Have you had a tendency to be self-absorbed?

What answers might be available to help you heal?

How does it feel to remember your innocence?

FINDING YOUR WAY

There is a catch to feeling love and joy; you also have to feel pain and anger.

Being in a healthy place is not that far off. To get there, however, you'll need to embrace your emotions.

If you feel like you're not able to have even that one moment of serenity, I want to give you hope.

I was there.

I remember thinking that if I could be happy for just one second a day, I would have hope.

My thoughts were so negative, so destructive.

I started doing my own scream therapy (even though I didn't know what it was actually called). When I first cleaned up from addiction, I used to pack up my oldest daughter and go to the beach in the winter because no one would hear me there. I would also go into the forest to scream.

The pain was so deep.

To find your way, you've got to be willing to…

…not care what people think.

…do whatever it takes to heal your life.

…get out of your comfort zone and release the pain in a healthy way.

Whatever your excuse is, make that your power to find a way.

I believe in you.

I see you.

I believe in you so much.

While that may sound strange coming from a book, this book is a reflection of my heart. It's from my heart to your heart.

Let this be your hope if you feel like you have none.

Think about it:

Have you had trouble embracing your emotions?

How could you benefit from not caring what people think?

How can you release the pain in a healthy way?

How can you turn your excuse into your power to find a way?

CHOOSING AGAIN

I'm going to invite you to make a choice.

Whether you believe it or not, the life that you're currently living is the result of your previous choices.

Now, you can choose again.

Maybe it's time to release the blame and take responsibility for the choices that you've made.

You can choose again.

I'm not talking about forgetting; I'm talking about forgiving. This includes forgiving yourself. Sometimes, when we work hard at forgiving others, we forget that we deserve forgiveness too.

I'm only asking for your willingness to allow a thought.

Consider the possibility that…

…the time is now.

…the healing begins now, while your eyes are opening and your consciousness is awakening.

…in this precise moment of being fully present, you have the ability to see things with complete clarity in vibrant colour.

Will you allow the thought?

Can you imagine having this clarity in your life every day?

Think about it:

How is the life that you're currently living the result of your previous choices?

How can you release the blame and take responsibility for the choices that you've made?

Have you worked hard at forgiving others and forgotten to forgive yourself?

THE PRESENT MOMENT

At every crossroads, there is a blessing.

The blessing begins when you say to yourself:

I never thought that I would be here at this time in my life.

What am I to do now?

That thought is a thought of clarity. It's an awakening. It shows you that you were asleep.

Now that you're in an awakened state, you can be fully present in your life.

When your mind is not in the past or the future but is in today, you can see all of the beauty of life.

You can…

…smell the flowers.

…take time to notice the leaves falling off of the trees.

…hear the birds chirping away in song.

…taste the vibrant colour of a classic car.

This is the perfection of the present moment.

Think about it:

When have you experienced a thought of clarity?

How did it show you that you were asleep?

How did it make you be more fully present in your life?

What is the perfection of this present moment?

THE POWER OF CONSCIOUS THOUGHT

Life can be amazing and extraordinary.

It can also be deceptive and manipulating.

Before you have a negative or positive thought about it, every situation is in a neutral state.

That's why it's important to be...

- Aware
- Open
- Willing

...as often as you can.

And because it always helps to be around people who can keep you on track, one of the best things you can do is to create or join a group of any kind.

You can also...

...have a code word of awakening to jolt you out of sleep consciousness.

...choose a ritual every morning, such as starting each day with an intention.

....choose people, dreams, and goals that keep you aligned with awakening.

Even if the only thing that you can focus on is to be grateful for…

- Your breath
- A soft blanket
- The clothes on your back

…pick that one thing, and push through the moment with your head held high for that second.

You can choose to live one day at a time.

And if that is still too long for you to make it through, then you can choose to live one second at a time.

You can choose to be present in every moment today.

You have the power to do whatever it takes.

I recommend that you pick a phrase — something that means a lot to you.

I'll always remember the two phrases that I developed as my go-to thoughts. They've become engrained in my mind through repetition.

Alana's Number One Life Phrase:

You can always give up, so why do it now?

Alana's Number Two Life Phrase:

You can get through this feeling for one more second. (Repeated until the feeling was gone.)

I would actually live from second to second.

It's a major gift to look back and see how far you've come in your life. I still have a ways to go, and that, to me, is now an exciting thought — not the overwhelming thought that it used to be.

Enjoyment, peace, and abundance are great experiences to strive for. You create your best life by being conscious of the thoughts that you think and the words that you speak.

Think about it:

How often are you around people who can keep you on track?

What would it take for you to be present in every moment today?

What phrase can you use as your go-to thought?

How can being conscious of the thoughts that you think and the words that you speak help you to create your best life?

Family or Group Discussion:

Take turns discussing your experiences, thoughts, and feelings about healing, then answer the following questions for yourself:

What is your next step toward creating the life you want to live?

When will you take that step?

Chapter Four
Clarity

DIRECTION

Do you think of clarity as a mysterious myth?

In the lineup at a fast food restaurant, it's easy to belt out, "I'd like a hamburger, fries, and a pop."

But when someone asks you what you want for your life, do you shrug your shoulders and say, "I don't know."

Do you think that it might be a good idea to…

…be clear on what you want for your life?

…have a direction for your life?

Think about taking a driving trip to a nice destination.

You enter the address into your navigation system, and the system tells you:

- Turn right.
- Turn left.
- Do this.
- Do that.

Wouldn't that be a great strategy for creating a successful life for yourself?

Think about it:

How clear are you about what you want for your
life?

If you had a GPS system for your life's journey,
what would it tell you right now?

CULTURAL CONDITIONING

Have you noticed that society is brainwashing you?

It began in your childhood with watching your parents. Whatever their emotional baggage, you saw it and took it on for yourself.

Or you did the exact opposite.

You had a reaction to every situation. Your reactions became your subconscious thoughts, and they got stuffed down deep.

Next, it was television that played a big part in the brainwashing.

It gave you subliminal messages, like:

Buy this now, whether you have the money or not.

Music also played a big part in the messaging.

(If you listen carefully to the words of your top ten songs, you might be amazed at what they're actually saying.)

Then, when you went to school, maybe the other children laughed at you.

In parent/teacher meetings, maybe they labeled you:

- Shy
- ADD
- Bully

In class, when the teacher asked you a question, and you put up your hand, excited to answer, maybe the teacher said, "No, that's wrong," and everyone laughed again.

After two or three tries, you wouldn't be so excited to keep offering answers, would you?

(Is it any wonder that public speaking has been found to be most people's number one fear—even above death?)

Think about it:

How have you noticed society brainwashing you?

How have your reactions become your subconscious thoughts?

What subliminal messages have you gotten from television and music?

What labels were you given in school?

SHINING YOUR LIGHT

I believe that personal development is the key to success.

When people ask me...

"Why are you doing another class?"

"Don't you know that you're being brainwashed?"

...I laugh and say, "I'd rather be brainwashed for success than brainwashed for failure."

Don't get me wrong.

The world is an amazing place.

People are also amazing.

I do, however, see dead souls walking around every day. These people may or may not want to change, and that has nothing to do with me.

I just don't want to join them again.

I'd rather go out and shine my light and bring my energy to every person I meet.

I hope that you'll do the same.

Think about it:

Are you being brainwashed for success or for failure?

Have you noticed the dead souls walking around?

What can you do to shine your light and bring your energy to every person you meet?

HAVING A PLAN

The clearer you can get about your…

- Purpose
- Vision
- Mission

…the clearer your direction will be.

The clearer your direction, the sooner you'll arrive at your destination.

Your end result is produced by:

- Having a plan
- Reverse engineering your life situation

This brings you clarity, at which point:

- The clarity moves you into action
- The action starts to produce profit

Clarity is power.

It's the power to control your destiny.

Ask yourself:

What do I like about my job?

What do I dislike about my job?

What excites me about life?

If money was no object, what would I do in my life?

If were to write my own eulogy today, what would I regret?

Think about it:

How clear are you about your purpose, vision, and mission?

Do you have a plan?

Have you ever reverse-engineered your life situation?

Are your actions producing profit?

How could having greater clarity give you greater control over your destiny?

What did you learn by asking yourself the questions about your job, your life, and your eulogy?

BUILDING YOUR LIFE

Have you ever made a blueprint for your life?

Blueprints are the design before the build.

As a former site superintendent in residential construction, I learned that every house begins with a blueprint.

Then come:

1. A solid foundation
2. The structure
3. The details

The process doesn't start with the walls, it starts with a plan.

Now, instead of building houses, I build lives. I love the life that I've built for myself, and I love to help others build their lives.

You can start building your life, right now, by asking yourself:

What are my five highest values?

What are my fields of interest?

How much time can I dedicate to my dream?

Think about it:

In what ways could you benefit from making a blueprint for your life?

What did you learn by asking yourself the questions about your values, your fields of interest, and dedicating time to your dream?

FINDING THE RIGHT RESOURCES

Are you asking yourself good questions about your life?

Asking good questions is the key to discovering what you want.

Then you can...

- Mind map
- Strategize
- Systemize
- Take a class

... or do whatever you need to do to get clear.

When I started asking the right questions, I found the resources I needed, and I know that there are resources out there for you too.

Finding the right resources often begins with finding the right person to help you push through to your desired lifestyle.

Think about it:

How could asking better questions support you in discovering what you want?

What if all the resources you need are out there waiting for you?

Have you found the right person to help you push through to your desired lifestyle?

GETTING OUTSIDE YOUR BOX

Have you ever noticed that most people live their entire lives inside their boxes of comfort, never realizing how small a portion of life they're experiencing?

My box was only about ten percent of what I'm experiencing in my life now, and each time I push through my comfort zone, I get to experience more of what's possible for me.

No matter how high your percentage gets, there are always going to be infinite possibilities outside of that box.

The following diagram shows what a typical comfort-zone box might look like, along with some of the expanded experiences available on the other side.

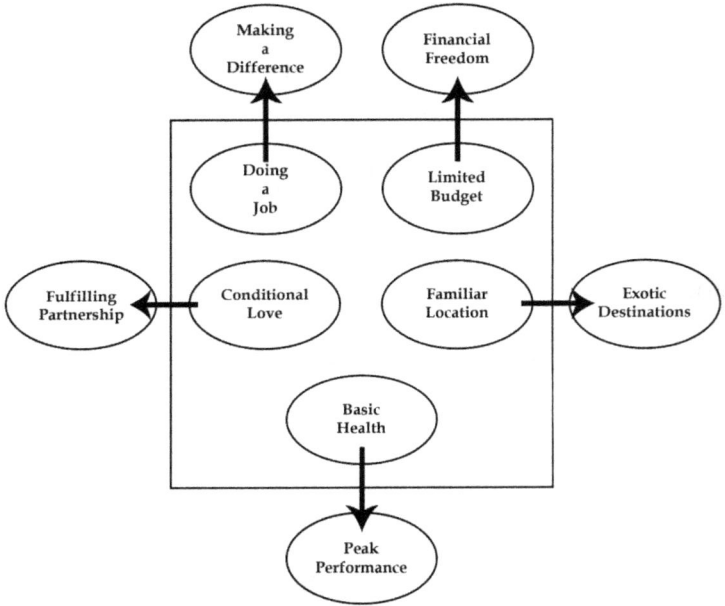

We all have our stories about why we don't do more, like…

"I don't have enough time."

"I don't have enough money."

"I can do it later."

…and so on.

If you're honest with yourself, you know that these are all just excuses, right?

When we say that we don't have enough time, money, or knowledge — or make any of the other excuses that we tell ourselves — we are allowing our fears to limit our lives.

But what are we really afraid of?

If you were to peek outside of your box (even for just a minute) what do you think you would see?

You might just catch a glimpse of your dream or your purpose.

I think you can handle that.

Think about it:

How long have you been living inside your current box?

What stories have you told about why you don't do more?

Have you had enough of fear ruling your decisions?

Are you ready to see what's out there for you?

VISUALIZING YOUR DESIRED LIFESTYLE

Here's a quick exercise:

1. Read the following instructions and questions.
2. Write out your answers on a piece of paper.
3. When you're done writing, close your eyes and visualize your dream life.

Note: This exercise is in the present tense. When you're writing it out, write it in the present tense, starting your sentences with phrases like:

I am...

I see...

I feel...

It's your life now. It's you getting up this morning. This is happening. You are living your desired lifestyle now.

Imagine that it's one year from today.

Imagine that money is no object.

What is your perfect life like?

What do you do every day?

Use all of your senses in this process.

What do you…

…hear?

…feel?

…taste?

…smell?

Feel the emotion.

What does the emotion feel like?

What does your house look like, and where is it?

What time are you waking up, and what do you do when you wake up?

What does your day look like?

Do you have…

…a private jet?

…a cook?

…a housecleaner?

What do you do at night?

Where are you?

How do you feel?

Think about it:

What did you learn from doing this exercise?

How can you use what you learned to help you achieve your desired lifestyle?

Family or Group Discussion:

Take turns discussing your experiences, thoughts, and feelings about clarity, then answer the following questions for yourself:

What is your next step toward creating the life you want to live?

When will you take that step?

Chapter Five
Action

YOUR LIFE PLAN

Did you know that your results will always be in direct proportion to the actions that you take?

This is a measurable fact.

Just as a company uses a business plan, you can use a life plan to help you determine the best actions to take. Once your life plan is in place, you can begin to break down your plan into chunk-sized portions.

You can use the chunk-sized portions to:

- Assign yourself tasks
- Get the tasks completed

There's a lot of structure that goes into putting your life's plan into action.

My process has included talking about:

- My past
- My gifts
- My passions

And the list goes on and on.

What will your process include?

Think about it:

How have your past results reflected the actions that you've taken?

How could benefit from breaking your life plan down into chunk-sized portions?

A POSITIVE STRATEGY

If the path to success were easy, then everybody would follow it.

While it may not be easy, the strategy to success is very simple.

It takes:

- Directedness
- Perseverance
- Consistency

That's why most people never go through the process. They get tired or frustrated, and they quit, just like they might quit an exercise program before they've achieved the results that they wanted.

When you exercise your body, the more you work a muscle, the stronger it becomes.

It's the same thing with a positive strategy. The more you do it, the easier it becomes.

Acting on one small new idea every day will create your breakthrough.

Each day, try doing one thing differently, such as:

- Edifying people instead of gossiping with them
- Speaking from a place of power instead of lack
- Being grateful instead of annoyed

Gratitude is free, and it creates peace within you because it's in alignment with your mind and heart.

Think about it:

Have you found yourself quitting before achieving the results you wanted?

What one small new idea can you act on today?

IT'S OKAY TO FAIL

Whether it seems like it or not, when you feel afraid because you're stretching beyond your comfort zone, you're actually in an exciting place.

If you relax with it, you'll notice that with every stretch beyond your comfort zone, you're reaching higher and higher states of consciousness.

Tell yourself:

This is my time.

I deserve it.

I've worked for this moment.

At the same time, understand that it's okay to fail.

I've started several traditional businesses, and not all of them were successful. From each business, I learned valuable lessons about what worked and what didn't work.

Statistically, only one out of seven businesses succeeds. One of the businesses I created, a successful million-dollar directional drilling company, is still running after seventeen years.

Do you think that would have happened if I had let the fear of failure stop me?

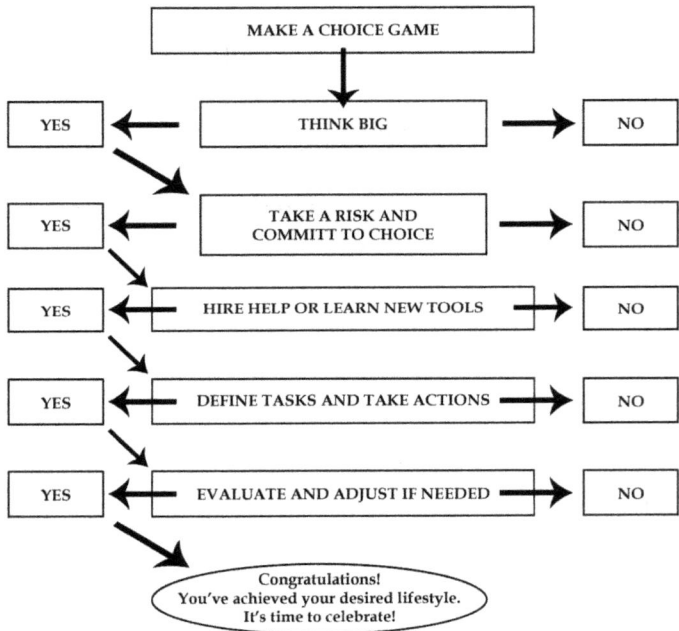

```
                    ┌──────────────────────────────┐
                    │     MAKE A CHOICE GAME        │
                    └──────────────────────────────┘
                                   │
                                   ▼
┌────────┐   ◄───   ┌──────────────────────────────┐   ───►   ┌────────┐
│  YES   │          │          THINK BIG           │          │   NO   │
└────────┘          └──────────────────────────────┘          └────────┘

┌────────┐   ◄───   ┌──────────────────────────────┐   ───►   ┌────────┐
│  YES   │          │      TAKE A RISK AND         │          │   NO   │
└────────┘          │     COMMITT TO CHOICE        │          └────────┘
                    └──────────────────────────────┘

┌────────┐   ◄───   ┌──────────────────────────────┐   ───►   ┌────────┐
│  YES   │          │  HIRE HELP OR LEARN NEW TOOLS │          │   NO   │
└────────┘          └──────────────────────────────┘          └────────┘

┌────────┐   ◄───   ┌──────────────────────────────┐   ───►   ┌────────┐
│  YES   │          │  DEFINE TASKS AND TAKE ACTIONS│          │   NO   │
└────────┘          └──────────────────────────────┘          └────────┘

┌────────┐   ◄───   ┌──────────────────────────────┐   ───►   ┌────────┐
│  YES   │          │ EVALUATE AND ADJUST IF NEEDED │          │   NO   │
└────────┘          └──────────────────────────────┘          └────────┘
```

Congratulations!
You've achieved your desired lifestyle.
It's time to celebrate!

NOTE:

When you play the Make a Choice game, if you choose "NO" and don't reach your desired lifestyle, remember that this is a game, and it can be played more than once. Take what you learned along the way, and get into the game again.

Think about it:

What would it be like to turn your fear into excitement when you stretch beyond your comfort zone?

What have you learned from your failures?

What can you learn by playing the *Make a Choice* game?

DO IT NOW

You don't have to be perfect to start.

You just have to start.

On my website, I have:

- My first e-book
- My first podcast
- My first video

What got me to do these was the thought:

If I don't take the action now, I may never do it.

The fear of never doing it far outweighed the fear of what people were going to think.

My reasons for putting each of these firsts on my website were:

- When I see how bad it is, I know that it can only get better.
- Now that I did it once, I know that I'll do it again.
- I want to inspire others to just do it.

Think about it:

What could you start right now if you didn't have to be perfect?

If you don't take the action now, will you ever do it?

What if your imperfections could inspire others?

OPEN YOUR HEART

In my experience, nothing is possible without God —
whatever that looks like to you.

Everyone has their own ideas of what God is from their
personal experiences and what they have been taught.

What if you were to let go of any ideas about God
other than having a belief in something greater than
yourself?

With God, there is no judgement; there is only love.

For centuries, many different religions have tried to tell
us what to think and do. My understanding is that if
we, ourselves, are not perfect, then we are not to judge
anyone else for not being perfect. Rather than going to
sleep in our anger toward others or ourselves, we are
to love ourselves and others.

When you recognize that to one degree or another,
we are all wounded people, and you stay conscious of
others and yourself, then forgiveness, healing, clarity,
and action are natural next steps.

Here's a good intention to set for yourself:

Each day, strive to do a little bit better.

The highest action of the heart and soul is service to
others. Whether your service is to your family, your

community, or the world is not important. To become your best self is to serve those who need you.

Wow!

What a gift to give to yourself and to the world.

Think about it:

Have you been asleep in your anger toward others or yourself?

To what degree has your life been about service?

What gifts could you share with yourself and others, and who do you think most needs those gifts?

DREAM BIG

There's a saying:

If your dream doesn't scare you, then it's not big enough.

When my dream scared me, I stood at the edge of my comfort zone and pushed right through.

Now, it's your turn.

I want you to dream big!

You can have it all.

I *know* you can!

And you don't have to do it alone.

I'm here for you.

Let's push through together!

Think about it:

Is your dream big enough to scare you?

How big can you go?

What if you really can have it all?

Are you ready to push through?

Family or Group Discussion:

Take turns discussing your experiences, thoughts, and feelings about action, then answer the following questions for yourself:

What is your next step toward creating the life you want to live?

When will you take that step?

Conclusion

THE LIFE YOU DESERVE

I hope that my story has assisted you in finding your way to the forgiveness, healing, and clarity you need to enjoy your life to the fullest. This book and its message are from my heart to your heart.

As your journey through these pages comes to an end, your journey to living your best life is just beginning. If you've taken the time to thoughtfully consider all that I've presented here, you may already have had a profound shift.

Now, why not go for another one?

Your life story is built in layers. When you continue to work with this material, you'll find yourself going deeper and getting clearer every time. Your answers to some of the questions will change, revealing the next level of your expanding consciousness, and your life experiences will reflect that expansion.

If you've been sleepwalking through life and telling an old, worn out story, now is the time to wake yourself up. Take the best of what you've learned here, and start putting it into action right away.

From this moment forward, the decisions you make and the actions you take will create your future.

What do you want that future to be?

You can sit around pondering all the possibilities and developing ideas about how to move forward, but without action, there will be no results. Getting out of your comfort zone and into action will bring you results every time.

One of my mentors once told me, "Just take one baby step at a time, and before you know it, your project will be complete."

Can you take one baby step at a time?

I know that you can.

I believe in you.

I know that with the right plan and the right support, you will create a life that you consider to be worth living.

Always remember that...

...you are a gift.

...you matter.

...you are here for a purpose.

...you can change your life.

...you make a difference.

There is no better time than right now to start living the life that you deserve to live.

THE GIFT OF GIVING

Don't you just love life's sense of humour?

When you're present in life, then life starts to make you laugh.

A couple of times a week, I catch something that I'm supposed to learn or notice.

I say to myself:

Aha! Thank you.

One day, as I was writing this book, I was thinking to myself:

Right now, I'm venturing so far out of my comfort zone that I'm feeling afraid something bad might happen.

This is one of those thoughts that gets me scaling the walls of my box to get back inside it as quickly as I can.

At this point in my life, however, the discomfort of getting back into my box is almost scarier than being on the outside.

So I keep going because…

…I'm committed to this process.

…I'm committed to myself.

…I'm committed to you.

I cannot ask you to push through your problems if I'm not willing to do the same. This is very important to me. You would not be reading this book right now if I had not been willing to face my fears and keep going.

Now, it's your turn.

I would love to hear what's happening in your life right now, and if you need an accountability partner to help you move through, then I am here for you. I believe that our path through life is about each and every person doing the best that they can for each and every other person.

If you'd like a push, then send me an email, and we can set up a time to talk, free of charge. I get excited when people succeed. Being here for you is how I give back for all the blessings that I have received.

Believe me when I say that when I get your email, it's a gift to me. Allow me the gift of hearing from you. You can send me success stories too. Just send an email.

I look forward to hearing from you.

www.PushyCoach.com

THE PUSH MOVEMENT

You are on this earth to experience unconditional love, freedom, and bliss.

Isn't it time to stop settling for less?

As a life and business coach, my expertise is in pushing people through their obstacles and retraining their brains for massive success. I guide people to set goals, and I give them someone to be accountable to. This moves them forward in their lives and careers.

You cannot do what you do not *know* to do. I shine a light on the part that you don't know about.

I call this the Push Movement.

This movement is for you if…

…you feel like you have not had a voice, and you need to get your confidence back up.

…you're ready to laser-focus your purpose and to design your life the way you see it in your mind.

…you want to retrain your thoughts and words, intentionally create the actions of your day-to-day activities, and overcome obstacles to get to your dream life.

Do you know the story of the four-minute mile?

Until the first person achieved it, athletes had been unable to run that fast.

Could that have been due to mindset?

Now, people shatter the record all the time.

Our lives are run by mindset.

Whatever barriers you may feel like you have, you can break through them and excel. There is only one thing holding you back, and that is you.

If you feel stuck in a job that you don't enjoy because you need the paycheque or the pension, then my goal is to bring you home.

Do you really think that pension is secure?
Imagine this scenario:

- You have stayed in a job for the pension.

- You retire with this pension and are just barely able to pay your bills.

- At the age of sixty-eight, you get a letter telling you that your pension has been cut by seventy percent.

Is that what you worked hard for all those years?

I'm not saying you shouldn't have your job and pension. I'm asking you to think about something else — passive income.

Passive income means:

- Making money while you're sleeping

- Not keeping all of your eggs in one basket

- Having three or four different streams of income coming in

It doesn't have to be built in a day. Just like savings, the work you put in compounds over time with a set plan and schedule.

If you're like most people, you may be thinking:

I don't have the time or the money to do that right now.

If that's what you're thinking, then that's exactly why you need to do it now.

How long have you been thinking and saying the same thing?

Has it been years?

If so, when do you think those conditions will change?

Instead of thinking about having no time or money, I want you to think about what your life would look like if you *did* have time and money.

If you have young children, do you realize that you only get eighteen summers with them before they'll be out in the same rat race that you've been in?

I'm asking these questions to give you something to think about. Maybe you've never asked yourself these kinds of questions before.

Why?

Because maybe no one ever told you to ask yourself good questions.

Most of us just watch what our parents do and follow suit. We watch what society does, and we do the same. I'm a bit of a rebel. Whatever society is doing, I do the opposite.

The financially free life is not for everyone. If it were, everyone would be doing it. It takes commitment. It takes asking for help and doing something toward your goals every day. It's not easy, but it is simple when you apply a few key behaviours like laser-sharp focus, perseverance, and tenacity.

If that life is for you, then your time is *now*.

I currently offer two programs:

1. **One-on-one coaching** to laser-focus your life and move you into action

2. **A one-day seminar** to rethink the mindsets that have been holding you back

Designing a Dream Lifestyle destination events will be coming soon.

To learn more, visit:

www.PushyCoach.com

ABOUT THE AUTHOR

Alana Leone is a loving mother and grandmother who believes in having it all.

After twenty years in the construction industry — during which she cared for her children at home *and* started a directional drilling company that is now worth over a million dollars — Alana discovered her life's long-forgotten passion to serve people in the field of personal development.

As a life and business coach, speaker, and author, Alana has found that the more people she helps to become their best, the more she is able to have everything she wants. Now known as the Pushy Coach, she is building her next empire, the Push Movement, which moves people into action creating their desired lifestyle.

Alana's mission is sharing freedom with the world.

Connect with Alana at:

www.PushyCoach.com

www.ingramcontent.com/pod-product-compliance
Lightning Source LLC
Chambersburg PA
CBHW072027040426
42447CB00009B/1768